POETIC *EXPERIENCES* WITH GOD:
From the Throne Room

L. I. S. A. ANDRADE-Thompson

Poetic *Experiences* with God:
From The Throne Room

COPYRIGHT @
Healing Rain
International 2019

POETIC EXPERIENCES WITH GOD: From The Throne Room

© Lisa Andrade-Thompson is the owner of this book and all its contents. No section of this book may be copied, reproduced or transmitted in any form or by any means, electronic or mechanical, including photocopying, recording, or by any information storage and retrieval system, without the written permission of the Copyright owner.

ISBN: 978-976-96317-0-0

Healing Rain International:
www.healingraininternational.com
healingraininspirationals@gmail.com

Chief Editor:
Doane Thompson

Assistant Editors:
Jasmin Lawrence
Brian Lawrence

Creative Design Director:
Dominique Condison-Thompson

Photographers:
Domeraki Media (Dominique Condison-Thompson)
All photographs taken by Domeraki Media
BriLawren Creative (Brian Lawrence)
Front Cover photograph taken by BriLawren Creative

Artistic Designers:
Brian Lawrence (front and back covers)
Brandon Hamilton (inside)

Foreword:
Bishop Christine Haber - Christine Haber Ministries

© *2019 Lisa Andrade-Thompson, All Rights Reserved.*

TABLE OF CONTENTS

DEDICATION 4
ACKNOWLEDGEMENTS 6
FOREWORD 10
PRELUDE 14

SEASON ONE: THE BIRTHING

A SPECIAL DAY 26
ALONE....but with GOD 30
HIS PRESENCE 36
FRIEND 40
WHAT IS LOVE? 44

SEASON TWO: THE FLOURISHING

THE WINDS OF CHANGE 52
WHAT IS YOUR SEASON? 57
WHO AM I? 61
YOU ARE GOD'S CHILD 68
ONLY YOU CAN BE YOU 73

SEASON THREE: THE BREAKING

FATHER 82
THE PROMISE 86
BROKEN... YET STILL CHOSEN 91
YOU ARE MY SHIELD 97

SEASON FOUR: THE LIVING

THE INNER LIGHT GLOWS 106
WATCH YOUR WORDS 110

SPEAK LIFE	115
MANIFEST	118
EPILOGUE	124
NOTES	128

DEDICATION

To all the people who have ever been hurt, discouraged, rejected, overlooked, depressed, entertained suicidal thoughts, had their dreams crushed, abandoned, forsaken, abused, struggled with self esteem issues or just traumatized by life's experiences. May this poetic experience bring you revelation, healing and deliverance from the influence that the enemy has over your mind, body and soul.

POETIC EXPERIENCES WITH GOD: From The Throne Room

ACKNOWLEDGEMENTS

WITH GOD ALL THINGS ARE POSSIBLE!

I wish to thank my dearest husband, Doane Thompson. Before the foundations of the earth the Lord predestined this Mighty Man of God to be the priest of my home, and for this I am eternally grateful. He is always pushing me to be greater than I think I am.

My three beautiful children, Dominique, Zahrah-Zayd and Israel, my three reasons to live, write, inspire and encourage.

My mom, for being the first one to look into my eyes and speak the promises of God without repentance or shame. She has always been one of my biggest cheerleaders in this journey called life.

My sister Sophia, the prayer warrior, her husband Dennis and my nieces Brittni-Shea and Shelby. I have seen in them, if I have ever missed it in life, the hand of God and how he prospers His own.

My sister Opal, her husband Robert and my niece Chante for their perpetual love.

The Late Apostle David G. Keane for giving me the foundation of the word of God that now governs my life's journey, and to his firstborn, Julie-Ann, for standing with me and encouraging me on this said foundation.

My mentor, Ordellene 'Jody' McCalla, who nurtured my spirit man for years, calling me into maturity and helping to steady my foundation in Christ.

My sister in Christ, Alysia Moulton White, who has never ceased to encourage me to publish my inspirational thoughts. Through her the Lord has encouraged and prodded me into my destiny.

My beloved spiritual leaders, Apostle Franz Fletcher and Pastor Dianne Fletcher for significantly contributing to my spiritual growth. I thank them both for the many opportunities to minister within the local body.

Evangelist Deborah Francis for obeying the voice of the Lord and always encouraging me to be who God has called me to be.

Brian Lawrence who assisted in bringing my vision to life and continues to encourage my creative works through his technical and moral support.

My special friend Bishop Christine Haber who never ceased to pray me through the good times and the bad, continuously speaking the promises of God over my life.

To all my support: Valerie Rennalls, Kadian Webb, Andrea McCurdy, Tanisha Alexander and

Tanya Goffe. Thanks for praying me up in the various seasons I have journeyed through.

FOREWORD

Lisa has gone from a glamorous airline agent to an entrepreneur who has been successful throughout her many endeavors and now life has thrusted Lisa into becoming an author.

Reading through her book, I can see the beauty of salvation in each new day and every breath she has taken, this great salvation has pulled her out of yesterday now marking the start of a great new beginning.

Her own life changing experiences have allowed her to create this anthology of poems in an articulate way that will change the mindset of all who read it. From the first time I met Lisa as a colleague in the travel industry she always served with excellence and I knew her infectious personality would take her very far. So today I am not surprised she has penned **"Poetic Experiences with God: From the Throne Room"** and I am excited for the journey this book will transition her on.

I was most proud of Lisa when she gave her life to Jesus Christ. At the time she was also a friend of my sister and I saw the phenomenal interest my sister had taken to intercede for Lisa's salvation. I knew from that time that she was extraordinary.

I began to agree, pray and fast for Lisa without her even knowing. Not long after I saw the miracle of her transforming before our very eyes. When she surrendered, God stepped in and the gift He deposited in her as a gospel singer manifested and began a revolution in the Kingdom of God, where many souls were won through her ministry.

In her own words from this book **"You will never know what the winds of change will bring, nothing ever remains the same."** *I personally have seen the wind of change in Lisa's life,* **"Each season moves you from level to level, always higher and higher yet** *attracting the devil. The Lord Himself determines your season."* Well said Lisa.

I am a witness to how the Potter's hand has molded this clay into a masterpiece. Indeed the journey she has been on and how she has displayed each of these poems inclusive of scriptures will surely change the lives and hearts of all who read this book. As previously mentioned this book is very timely.

Our destiny is in the hand of God and when the appointed time comes no man can stop it. I continue to pray for you my sister in Christ. I am proud of you.

God bless all who read.

Habakkuk   2:3
"For the revelation awaits an appointed time, it speaks of the end and will not prove false. Though it lingers, wait for it, it will certainly come and not delay."

BISHOP CHRISTINE HABER
CHRISTINE HABER MINISTRIES

PRELUDE

As a youngster I always visited a church close to home and I never really took the visits very seriously. I grew up in the Anglican faith where doctrines were very different. I constantly searched yet never found what I truly needed. I tried so hard to find myself because all those years I thought I knew who I was. I was the epitome of a social butterfly hung out with friends and partied ever so often trying to fill that empty space on the inside of my soul.

My party days were about to embark on a sudden halt. Every day at my airline job I would be invited to midday prayer by a newly hired employee who became a close friend. I would often repel the consistent invitation even though I would always promise that I would attend. My excuse for not making it was always that there were passengers in the queue to be processed for the flight and I had to ensure they were taken care of.

One particular day my very persistent friend Angelie invited me again and decided she would wait on me, refusing to leave me behind. It was evident to all that the Lord had planned for me that day to walk into His presence. It was packaged so attractively by the Holy Spirit that I could not resist the beauty of the Lord and Angelie had the pleasure of leading me in a repentant prayer.

It followed through as one fateful Sunday subsequent to my experience at work; that the church I often visited and never took seriously began calling my name in the Spirit. I answered the call and visited the church that morning. The Praise and Worship and the sermon that day were just what the Holy Spirit ordered. The ministering Pastor gave an altar call and I felt the tugging in my heart but still remained quietly in my seat. As the Pastor continued to minister the tugging became overwhelming as if someone was pulling me out of my seat and toward the altar. I eventually had no choice but to respond to the call, so I went to the altar and cemented my commitment to the Lord again sealing it in eternity that very Sunday.

After this double take (work and church intervention) the real warfare began. I began to learn the difference between the voice of the Lord and the voice of the enemy. Being raised in a separate faith (from what I believe now) I was led to believe that Blessing at birth and confirmation at puberty suggested that I was saved and responsible for my sins.

This allowed me to constantly shun baptism by immersion. The enemy played games with my mind and kept me at that place for a full two (2) years before that stronghold was broken. I was finally baptized on February 4, 2001 by divine setup totally orchestrated by God through a man of God, Elder Francis Hill.

It was 'A Special Day' when the Lord brought me into the newness of Himself. My Christian journey began and it was often walked 'Alone ....But with God'. I learnt that you had to crucify flesh in order to experience 'His Presence' and in doing this you would eventually find out who a true 'Friend' really is. After knowing God and experiencing His love you will be able to testify of that love 'What Is Love.' The word of God in Romans 8:38-39 reveals to us that there is no height nor depth no length nor breadth that can separate us from the divine love of God.

On your journey you will always experience 'The Winds of Change' and it will become more and more necessary to ask yourself 'What is your Season?'
The Lord brought me many times to the point where I would question my very existence and I struggled with who I was, I always believed that I was less worthy than everyone around me. I would oftentimes ask the Lord

'Who Am I?' and I would hear His reassuring voice saying, 'You Are my Child.' These words of encouragement would constantly reassure me that He had bestowed upon me a supernatural and unique anointing to do His work.

Family and friends would always enjoy my company and would often encourage me to be myself and they would say 'Only You Can Be You' Lisa, but society taught us otherwise. Strive to be like the divas, the models and the beauty queens that you see in magazines. I tried all that and I realized that I did not want to be like anyone but myself. To this end I endeavoured to be different for the Glory and honour of God.

As my journey continued I learnt much more about my heavenly 'Father' about His ways and His commands and how everything about Him was by His word. There always had to be a sacrifice before you could walk into any of "The Promises" of God. Throughout my Christian walk I have been hurt and broken, rejected and reassured, scorned and elevated, yet my Abba Father would remind me that despite my roller coaster journey I was 'Broken…..Yet Still Chosen'.

Feeding on the undiluted word allowed the very word to perform a major bypass surgery on my stony heart where my brokenness became my platform, my stepping stone to victory in Him. I believed in His word and I believed that He was "My Shield", my ever present help in the time of need.

Many times I ended up bowed down in despair with my face to the floor but because I learnt how to remind myself of the Greater 'He that is within me than He that is in the world' I had to let 'My Inner Light Glow' where I lived a life of self motivation constantly reminding myself that life and death is in the power of the tongue, 'Watch your words ..for your words watch you.'

I learnt through experience that your words not only had a weight but it had dunamis power to perform what it was sent to do. The truth is, we were made in His image and formed in His likeness and the same power that resides in Him resides in us. Therefore in the beginning when He spoke the word '*let there be light,*' the power of His spoken word caused the light to permeate the darkness.

Believe it or not we have this same power residing in our spoken word so in all situations no matter how bad it looks and how tough it gets we must "Speak Life" and in this the will and the way of God for our lives must "Manifest" before our very eyes.

I never fully understood the journey my life took from a youthful age. I always thought life would have a lot of beautiful and encouraging lessons to offer. But as I walked the journey of life I found that even though life offered beautiful and encouraging lessons there were some really hard lessons that would also come your way.

At the end of the day the most important lesson I learnt is that I should live a confessed life and He would work me through every obstacle and challenge that I may face. Although no one has the ability to hide anything from God there is a beauty in living a confessed life before Him. Speak out and confess those sins, flaws, inhibitions, just about everything to Him and He finds pleasure in walking you through life every step of the way.

Inspired by the Holy Spirit these poetic experiences will expose you to a new revelation of our Abba Father. Allow it to unfold; unfold in your heart and mind as you are healed, delivered, set free from that which easily besets you. Dust off the mess, stand on the word of God and walk out your purpose. Remember the steps of a righteous man are ordered. Indulge and become a part of my **Poetic Experiences With God: From the Throne Room**.

A SPECIAL DAY

Every day in God's eyes is a special day. A thousand years to us is one day to our Abba Father. Before we were formed in our mother's womb we were predestined for greatness and our Abba Father orchestrated every step of our journey before the very foundation of the earth for His pleasure.

We were formed in His image and created in His likeness for the sole purpose of worshipping Him. Disobedience was the device that made us take the fall from God's presence and it was because of our disobedience that sin was born in our hearts and minds.

When our Abba Father conceived us in His thoughts it was before the foundation of the world was established... before He formed us He foreknew us... before He foreknew us He set us apart. Refuse to accept any negative the enemy has to speak into your lives because the fact that you were born means you were predestined.

In following hard after God a special day will also come when we confess the Lord as our personal Saviour and openly repent of our sins so we become born again. This special day is recognized in the heavenlies where angels rejoice when one comes to know the Lord. Our Abba Father has set aside a special day for each and every one of us, to walk boldly into His Presence.

A SPECIAL DAY

Today is a special day
Because you were born on this day
God predestined this day
Because He had you in His thoughts

This day was created especially for you
May all your desires come true
May you live a life pleasing to the King
And surrender to Him everything

Today is a special day
Because you were born again on this day
The Lord will enrich you this day
And make all things go your way as you surrender
your will to His

This day was created especially for you
May all your desires come true
May He fill your life with treasures
And may He will unto you all your pleasures
As you are born again you become a new creation
A Special day created just because of you……

Through your rebirth ...A promise is born!!

Jeremiah 1:5 Ecclesiastes 3:2

Copyright @ May 26, 2005

ALONE....but with GOD

Through your season of Birthing, there will be times when you may feel alone yet you are in a crowded room. Your experiences will sometimes attempt to isolate you from everything positive in your life. There will come a time in your journey when you will be bombarded with negative thoughts and manifestations where you may become extremely overwhelmed with emotional turmoil, but God.

The enemy will attack your very belief in God with the aim of discrediting the power of your Abba Father.

There will be times when you become situation driven and expect to gain happiness from particular situations and relationships in life, but as you mature you will realize that you find less happiness in people and situations and come to the revelation that true joy is really achieved through knowing the Lord.

All the family and friends that you have sometimes seem to be at a distance while you seem to be all alone. Your birthing is on the way yet life seems to be on a spiral downturn and you cannot retrace why or even know how long it will be before you rise. Only God can comfort you through these times.

You may even get to a place where you feel the need to withdraw from the very thing you are anointed to do. You may feel as if you are under attack, but the fact often is that our Abba Father allows events to occur so you can meet Him at His place where He has you all to Himself. At His place is where He is free to minister to your spirit and birth you into your season.

Never be intimidated by what you think is the wiles of the enemy because it is often the hidden hand of God carrying you away as He seeks to impart to you in His presence.

Alone …but with God

The room grows still
As your thoughts recollect the day's events
You glance to your right then to your left
You are all alone in a crowded room….yet you feel a presence

Life takes you through a spiral of events
It has its ups it has its downs
There are times when you are even sure about giving up
There is no one around who even cares or discerns to encourage you
You are officially on your own …yet you feel a presence

The financial pressures of life press you in
The pain of a lost relationship or lack of it gets you down
The hurt of the past lingers still
The complications of the present cause you to become grim

You retreat into the shell of protection you have created
Just to be alone…yet you still feel a presence

Disappointments constantly bombard your very existence
But that is because your hope is connected to the wrong life line
Things may always seem to get you down
But 'seem' has no truth to it, it's a perception, it's a feeling
So you drift away again into that place of aloneness, wanting to be alone
But a presence is still present

No one to share your thoughts with
No one to trust with your innermost cares
No one you can talk to without feeling insecure in what you have shared
You fall prey again and enter that place where the enemy tries to bond you
Sift you and trap you in that place called aloneness

POETIC EXPERIENCES WITH GOD: From The Throne Room

Even in this state a presence is still present

But Trust in the Lord with all your heart and lean
not to your own understanding
And in all thy ways acknowledge Him and He
will direct your path
Because His word says He will never leave you
nor forsake you
He says His angels encamp around those who fear
Him
He says He upholds you with His righteous right
hand
His right hand of dominion and power
He says He that is within you is greater than He
that is in the world
He says you are the apple of His eye
He says when you seek Him with all your heart
you shall find Him
He says when you call upon His name He shall
answer
He says His ear is attentive to your cry
He says He is ever present in times of trouble

He says no weapon formed against you shall prosper
He has commanded His angels to stand guard around you

Can you really be alone?
You may feel alone…
But the presence is His presence that has always been there
In your heart, flooding your mind, teaching your soul, governing your spirit
Alone……but with God!!!!!!!

Proverbs 3:5-6 Psalm 91:11 Zechariah 2:8
Isaiah 41:10, 54:17
Copyright @ June 16, 2005

HIS PRESENCE

You never really experience anything in life until you have experienced the very presence of God. This is not only encountered while the congregation is at the highest point in Praise and Worship.... It does not only happen when singing your favourite song.... Not even when your favorite Praise Leader or Preacher is leading in worship or preaching the undiluted word. His presence can be experienced in quietness or even in the midst of a crowd.

For some it can happen during your personal worship and prayer time. My first experience with the presence of God was shortly after I became a Christian and I was at home doing my devotions and playing my CeCe Winans CD' 'Alabaster Box' to be precise. During the worship I was elevated to a supernatural realm where in an open vision I knelt at the feet of Jesus. I saw His feet literally before me and as I tried to raise my head to see more of Him, a supernatural power kept me in a bowed position just worshipping...oh Holy, oh Worthy are You Lord.

This vision even now keeps my life in perspective because I know He is REAL **'Really Everywhere and Living'**. This vision revealed to me that wherever He leads me in life, whatever He allows me to go through, whichever highway He takes me on, my place will always be at His feet. At your Father's feet His eyes watch over you, His love surrounds you, His hands are constantly upon you, your head is just an arm's length away and most importantly He always feels you at His feet.

The presence of God is truly experienced through self denial. This is when we decide to give up our kingdom for His Kingdom. The piece "His Presence" was written in my spirit by the Lord during one August afternoon in 2002. While I was sleeping He woke me up and commanded me to write. I obeyed and here is "His Presence".

HIS PRESENCE...

Is as still as a dark night. It is pure, it is real, it is love, it is joy

It is freedom to express, it is purity of thought

It is comfort, it is understanding, it is piercing your very soul

It is where your spirit has an encounter with its spirituality

It is lenient, it is harsh, it is favour, it is foundation

It is forever, it is ever present, it is alive, it is real, it is honourable, it is holy

It creates harmony, it mends brokenness, it increases faith

It leads, it inspires, it teaches, it listens

It loves without condition, it cleanses, it promotes excellence

It gives without asking, it produces self confidence, It gives security, it bears burdens, it breaks yokes, it erases fear

It has no colour, it has no favourites, it gives promises, it fulfills promises

It calls, it equips for the call, it heals, it delivers, it resurrects
It rewards, it is intense, it refreshes, it endures
It appoints, it is endless, it provides…It is simply perfect…..
It is the **Presence of God!**

Exodus 33:14 Psalm 16:1, 31:20 Acts 2:28
Copyright@ August, 2002

FRIEND

A friend is always a friend to the end. Learn that not everyone who smiles with you can be called a friend, not everyone who talks with you can be called a friend, not all those you invite to your home can be called friend; not all who make themselves familiar can be called friends.

A true friend first has to be ordained by God. True friends never die is what many say; they stick with you through thick and thin. They cry when you cry, they laugh when you laugh; they are always willing to tell you the truth and stand by you in the rough times.
They share your dreams and encourage you to pursue them, they cover your tracks of errors, they lend a helping hand; they encourage you through your tears, they mature with you through the years; they speak positively into your life, always reassuring, always uplifting.

A true friend is a friend to the end regardless of whatever difficulties may come. People enter your life generally for a reason, a season or a lifetime but the best part to note is… if a mortal friend can accomplish all or most of this, what says our Abba Father.

Can you imagine what He thinks about us as His friend…God is a lifetime FRIEND! As the word of God says in John 15:13 - Greater love hath no one than this; that He laid down His life for His friends.

FRIEND..*Friends are forever!*

Faithful – always faithful to God and to your relationship with Him as commitment adds a whole new meaning to that relationship and how He will allow you to grow in Him.

Rebukes – the Holy Spirit will always emphasize and reinforce your strengths and reveal your weaknesses in order to help you become a better you.

Intercedes - is what Jesus does on our behalf seated at the right hand of the father always seeking for our good.

Encourages – the Holy Spirit is always on spot to encourage us in His word and with the confidence knowing that He is ever present training us to always have a positive attitude.

Nurtures – the Holy Spirit is the master trainer in our spiritual development as well as our emotional maturity.

Directs – the Holy Spirit always gives good and positive directions throughout our valuable life lessons. As the word says the steps of a righteous man are ordered, He constantly directs our steps.

Proverbs 17:7, 18:24, 27:6, 10
Copyright © January 19, 2004

WHAT IS LOVE?

It is because of His love why we were created in His Image and formed in His likeness. We were truly created to love and worship God. It is through this nature that we deeply desire to love and be loved. We have all at some point in our lives experienced true love and even then it can still be an unsatisfying search to fill a void that we have.

The only way you can experience true love is in Christ. As you explore life you will find that love is endless; it has unending facets to it and if not careful it can seem as if it is not true. However, the truth is, Love is a purity of expression coming from deep within that you give because you are unable to hide it.

It must be expressed for you to be fulfilled. Love cannot be expressed only by words, love is infinite, love is God, love is a doing word…it has to be demonstrated. Love is far greater than a mere feeling; it is a commitment and it needs to be constantly worked on.

However, for God it is unconditional, He loves us regardless of how we are because He created us out of a deep passionate love for us. The love of God for us never ends, it goes on to infinity.

The word of God in Romans 8:38-39 says, **"For I am persuaded, that neither death, nor life, nor angels, nor principalities, nor powers, nor things present, nor things to come, nor height, nor depth, nor any other creature, shall be able to separate us from the love of God, which is in Christ Jesus our Lord"**

I was inspired to pen this when a more than special man walked right into my life. He eventually, at God's will became the priest of my home. I am persuaded that my Abba Father created him specifically for me, to suit my every need as well as to keep me on the path to Christ. His ways were Godly and he demonstrated every aspect of the piece "What is Love". He knew how to love deeply and passionately as well as love without expecting anything specific in return. The qualities which His Spirit emanated showed me that despite my flaws there was one created just for me. He demonstrated true reverence and love for God. He was intimate with the word of God as how the word of God is intimate with the pages of the Bible. He was a true man of God.

If this depth of feeling could emerge from a mortal being what says God....this gave me a greater revelation of how God feels about me His child. Love is truly the greatest gift of all time.

WHAT IS LOVE?

Love is GOD and GOD is love, Love is true and love is life
Love overshadows flaws, Love understands
Love creates, Love energises
Love surrounds, Love embraces

Love never leaves, Love is selfless
Love is pure, Love is spiritual
Love is honest, Love is fulfilling
Love laughs, Love gives

Love sacrifices, Love is joy
Love is peace, Love covers a multitude of sins
Love is encouraging, Love dedicates everything
Love is unconditional, Love radiates

Love heals, Love promotes
Love is faithful, Love is kind
Love endureth all things
Love is everything, Love never fails
Love is the greatest gift of all time!

I Corinthians 13:4-7, Proverbs 10:12 I

Peter 4:8

Copyright @ January 19, 2004

THE WINDS OF CHANGE

Life is ever changing…..change is upon the wind. The only thing in life which remains constant is change. It is so surprising to us the changes that come our way yet God knows them all. Always learn to discern a change of wind in your life because sometimes the wind changes and we are left holding on to something that has done its season in our lives. Life is ever changing and change is constantly upon the wind.

Movements spiritually - there is a time for maturity. Movements physically - there is a time to shift so you can walk into your blessing. Movements financially - there is a time to be blessed by God Himself. Movements emotionally - there is a time to experience some emotional growth where we mature and rise above our stumbling blocks to the next level. Movements generally are caused by "The Winds of Change".

Some survive while some fall behind due to their lack of the ability to quickly transition. The Winds of Change will never cease to blow and even if you are not ready for it …it is ready for all to know that change has come.

All winds of change are orchestrated by God and He allows them to blow in our lives at seasonal times. Each change has its purpose and our destiny attached to it. Without unexpected winds of change we would remain complacent and not pursue our purpose in life or even attempt to walk in intimacy with God, seeking His revelation.

The piece "Winds of Change" came into my life on the specific occasion when my family and I had to relocate, because the house we called home would in a few weeks become rubble. Even though it was for the better it was at first extremely uncomfortable for me because I loved that old house…..but as it states it was pretty old so this was a move I had to make regardless of how I felt about it. A contractor signed a deal with my mom to demolish and reconstruct townhouses where we would eventually reside again.

While relocated, in the Stony Hill environs an unexpected wind of change blew in my direction. Sickness was at my doorstep and I was forced to do major surgery and was off from work for a period of six weeks. This wind, as unexpected as it was, led me to have a greater and deeper relationship with the Lord as I depended on Him for my healing, often on my back looking up not only for healing but also for direction and guidance.

I learnt that not all winds should be despised because they all have their own unique purpose in our lives. Ready or not you must embrace **"The Winds Of Change"**.

POETIC EXPERIENCES WITH GOD: From The Throne Room

THE WINDS OF CHANGE

A cool calm night, Almost as dark as black
A soft cool wind, barely there
Nothing is ever the same
Change is upon the wind

Nothing is ever the same, Life is ever changing
Some for good, some for bad
Some to our surprise, sometimes to our demise
It is never the same
Change is upon the wind

A strong wind a rough night
As windy as a stormy day
It takes, it makes, it orders change
Anything in its path will never stay the same
No change takes God by surprise
Change is upon the wind

He orchestrates them all, He reveals them all
He is in control of them all, Trust in HIM
Because you will never know what
THE WINDS OF CHANGE will bring

L.I.S.A. Andrade-Thompson

Nothing ever remains the same

Change is upon the wind….

Proverbs 3:5-6 Ecclesiastes 11:5

John 3:8

Copyright @ February, 2004

WHAT IS YOUR SEASON?

Ecclesiastes 3:1. There is a time for everything under the sun and we must grow to recognize this. As the natural seasons change when it is due in the scheme of time they demonstrate their specific characteristics. Though one season naturally flows after another, they all possess different manifestations.

However, as it is in the natural so it is in the spirit. When seasons are changing they change without mans approval, Abba Father is the governing authority that dictates the reason for each season. We are often times forewarned and sometimes we are not. However, what we must note is that seasons will continue until the end of time and we will have no choice but to learn to adjust accordingly.

Seasons sometimes out last people but God's plans and purposes must be fulfilled, so even if someone exits a season of your life for one reason or another the Lord will appoint another to allow

His plans to remain. There is purpose in our pain as much as we detest going through it all. Regardless of what season it is, always know your season and discern the newness.

WHAT IS YOUR SEASON?

There is a reason for your season
Winter, Autumn, Summer, Spring
God is a God of perfect timing

Each season moves you from level to level
Always higher and higher yet attracting the devil
The Lord himself determines your season
While you decide how to reason the season
Your season will tell you about you
Your season will tell you what is due
Only God can change or alter the seasons
Because He holds the keys and the reasons

You have to praise Him through whatever season
Because this is your only hope
He sustains you, He maintains you
He restores you, He reassures you
He shapes you, He makes you
Always into someone new and improved
Through every season that you go through
Many don't make it through

They allow their situations to dictate the wrong
things to do
But God said, He will give you a garment of
praise for the spirit of heaviness
And the oil of joy for mourning
God lines each season in your life
With His hope, peace, joy and understanding

He reveals to you parts of your walk through His
Spirit
Calamities will come and they will go
But walk with God through every season
Because He always has a reason for every season
Winter, Autumn, Summer, Spring
God plans all your seasons don't ever doubt
Him!!!!

Spring – *The Birthing*
Summer – *The Flourishing*
Autumn – *The Breaking*
Winter – *The Living*

Ecclesiastes 3:1-8
Copyright @ June 12, 2005

POETIC EXPERIENCES WITH GOD: From The Throne Room

WHO AM I?

The winds of life will buffet you from all sides yet you need to know who you truly are. People will always oppose you especially when you are anointed of God. In some areas of your life you have to display a high and constant level of confidence. You can only truly find yourself in the Lord.

Your confidence comes from the Lord not from man or any other source and God is the foundation of who you really are. You were birthed from His Spirit from the beginning of creation, created in His image and formed in Hs likeness.

Who are you? Who are you really? You should know who you are and have confidence in who God has made you solely because you were created in His image and likeness. This is more spiritual than physical because we were created with God's DNA hence our identity is confirmed with His Holy word. Who Am I? You will be tested by the word of God. Whatever the word of God says about you will train you in weathering those tests that come your way, believe in who He has declared you to be.

When man sees you they must see the God in you and that is who you are. You are defined by the word of God not by your environment, job title, name or status in life. Who are you? If you were someone else and had the chance to meet yourself would you want to meet you? If your answer is no then you will have some work to do.

We can only truly find ourselves in the Lord because it is by His word that we are defined and not by what we think of ourselves or what other people think about us. Others are always laden with opinions but it is the Lord's definition and declaration of you through His word that truly counts. The Lord has defined you through His word so stand firm in it, walk in confidence with it, and run up into the enemy's camp declaring it in boldness. Then, you can confidently express who you truly are by the Spirit of God.

WHO AM I?

I am who God says I am
Not who you say I am
I am fearfully and wonderfully made
This is who He says I am

I am a Royal priesthood
I am a Holy Nation
I am a Peculiar person
This is who He says I am

I am the apple of His eye
I am the righteousness of God
I am the temple of the Holy Spirit
This is who He says I am

I am joint heir with Christ Jesus
I am a child of the Most High King
I am more than a conqueror through Christ Jesus
This is who He says I am

I am the head and not the tail
I am the lender and not the borrower

I am blessed coming in I am blessed going out
This is who He says I am

I have Christ living in me; therefore
I have the authority to do anything
I have the power to overcome everything
I possess the Spirit which guides all things
This is who He says I am

I am predestined by God; therefore
I am chosen, I am an original
I am consecrated…set apart; therefore
I am anointed, I am highly favoured of God
I am blessed beyond measure

This is who He says I am
Not who you say I am
Who does He say you are?
Can you confidently ask

WHO AM I?

POETIC EXPERIENCES WITH GOD: From The Throne Room

1Peter 2:9 Isaiah 61:1, Romans 8:17, 37
Psalm 139:14

Copyright @ March 17, 2005

YOU ARE GOD'S CHILD

Life has many roads, detours, dead ends, soft shoulders, cul-de-sacs and highways but you should always be led by God wherever he chooses to lead if you are a child of God. Your steps are ordered by God because he said in this word that the steps of a righteous man are ordered. He said no height, no depth, no principality, no power, can separate us from the love of God. This simply means, He will move mountains and burst open prison gates for His children.

His word also says no eye has seen nor ear heard nor has it entered into the heart of man what He has in store for those who love Him… but he has revealed it to us through His spirit. On life's journey always remember that whichever steps you take they are ordered. Whatever comes your way in life will work together for your good because you love the Lord and you are called according to His purpose.

Just like an earthly father watches over his children to protect them from walking certain roads in life, what more our heavenly father who governs all things in the vast universe will do. There are unique situations that will be set up for you with the aim of destroying you but what the enemy meant for bad the Lord allows it to work out for your good.

I remember transitioning jobs in 2005. I moved from the airline business to enter the hotel business. This was a great move for me as it was a good promotion moving from Sales Agent at the airline to Director of Sales and Marketing of a prominent hotel in Kingston. I had no idea I would have been called for such an opportunity after submitting my application. This revealed to me that when God has a planned road for you to travel nothing or no one has the ability to stop it, not even you.

As a child of God there are many promises that the Lord has recorded in His word about you and through his word you reap your inheritance. In all things, one of my constant confessions is "no weapon formed against me shall prosper and every tongue that rises against me in judgment shall be condemned because this is my heritage."

Walk in your God given authority and rise above every obstacle that is set before you to deter or distract you. Remember you are not your own you are bought with a price. Every gift that you receive from your Abba Father is not for your benefit but to build up the kingdom of God.

YOU are GOD'S CHILD

You are God's Child
You walk in authority
Always affecting the majority
You are God's Child
You are a King

You are God's Child
You know the Kingdom secrets
You possess spiritual power
Always guiding you through every hour
You are God's child
You are a King

You are God's child
You can call all things into being
As He keeps His hand upon you
And His love surrounding you
You are God's child
You are a King

You are God's child
There is nothing that separates you from His love

He leads your way and directs your path
You were not created for you but created to be used
You are God's child
You are a King

Romans 8:17, 38-39   1 Peter 2:9

Copyright @ May 26, 2005

ONLY YOU CAN BE YOU

From before the foundations of the Earth, from before the light permeated the darkness, from the Earth was without form and void, you were on His mind, in His Spirit and you were like none other. The very day that was pre-ordained for you to be birthed into this world was created especially for you.

You were never created to be a part of this world and be a duplicate of anyone. You were created to be a design original, no carbon copy, no imitation. Even the most identical of twins are still different in nature, character traits, likes and dislikes.

When God manifested you in His thoughts He was very specific with your design and purpose in mind.

Can you fathom a God so precise in His creation? Our limited way of thinking cannot conceive that level of planning. You were handmade, you were crafted, you were purposed and you were brought forth in love.

As you learn to love and celebrate you, come to realize and appreciate your uniqueness. Everything, down to the colour of your skin, was planned by God. You are not a mistake. You are not an afterthought. You are fearfully and wonderfully made in His image.

I remember my high school days at Wolmers Girls. I had a very special friend who in my eyes reflected a well behaved Christian young lady who I wanted to emulate, even though I had popularity in my hands. I admired her so much that I thought to myself 'I should just be like her'. Little did I know she was also looking at me and thinking to herself 'if I could only be like Lisa, loved by all'.

It wasn't until years after when we met again in church and rekindled our friendship that we realized that we had similar thoughts of each other.

After all of those immature thoughts we grew to realize that we were created to be ourselves and self love was the ultimate gift from God to fulfill purpose. God created a special package and called it by your name, gave it your claims and no one can ever be the same as who He created you to be. Love yourself, be yourself and live your best life in Christ because He has put a lot of thought into you.

POETIC EXPERIENCES WITH GOD: From The Throne Room

ONLY YOU CAN BE YOU

You were made you
God never made two
No one smiles like you
No one does the things you do
You are the apple of His eye
Only you can be you

Only you can be you
The unique things you say
Your ability to make someone's day
Your calling is for you
You are His masterpiece
No one can ever be like you

The path that you walk
The divinity with which you talk
Just the way you are
He has made you a Star
There is only one of you
Only you can be you
You should enjoy glancing around
Because only one of you can be found

POETIC EXPERIENCES WITH GOD: From The Throne Room

The way you think, your taste in things
The way you were designed, only you can be you

You are His masterpiece
He put a lot of thought into you
He created you before He formed you
Before the foundations of the earth
You are His original

Your purpose is set
Your path is planned
Your steps are ordered
Your goals are to be had….
But only you can achieve them
Because they specifically belong to you

Created for you to carry them through
Celebrate your creativity
Don't deny your identity
Burst forth into your spirituality
In what He has created you to be and do
Because…..at the end of it all
Only you can be you.

Psalm 139:14 Proverbs 16:9

Jeremiah 1:5

Copyright @ June 4, 2005

POETIC EXPERIENCES WITH GOD: From The Throne Room

SEASON THREE

The Breaking

POETIC EXPERIENCES WITH GOD: From The Throne Room

FATHER

Who is like a father, who can truly love and nourish like a father can. A true father is one who loves his children unconditionally. He would move mountains at the drop of a hat, if it were possible.

My earthly father showered me with everything he thought I needed. As I grew older he gave me the best advice and guidance about everything I could think of in life. My father was Cuban born and was seventeen years older than my mom.

Although he was not the youngest most agile dad, this never stopped him from showering me with love and affection. I was officially a daddy's girl and I strongly believe this contributed to the caliber husband that the Lord has blessed me with.

There was nothing my father wouldn't do for me. He was my strength, my motivator, my protector, my mentor and most of all he was my friend. My entire life growing up my father would discipline me yes but never by beating. I remember once I was rude and he decided to discipline me with the belt. It took me weeks to recover from the thought that my dad would actually punish me in this manner, but so it is in the natural so it reflects in the spiritual.

God is the ultimate father and he is one who stands by His word. If my earthly father could represent so much positive in my life including the chastening, then what says my Heavenly Father. He is the author and the finisher of my faith. He speaks into my life and watches over every word to perform it. He leaves no stone unturned to ensure I walk in my purpose.

FATHER

Father and Friend
- One who is always there.
- A mighty man a King
- One who seeks council from the Lord.
- One you can trust with your thoughts.
- One who loves to give of himself.

Available to be used by God for His Glory
- A man whose will is totally surrendered to God.
- A man whose flesh does not dominate his actions.

The head of his house
- He recognizes God as the head of his home.
- The priest of his home.
- He is the 'man' of the 'woman'.
- He is the main decision maker.
- He sets the standard for his family.
- His family holds Godly priority.

***H**onours God in all things*

- He honours God in everything he does and says.
  - He maintains prayer with the family.
  - He allows God to guide his decisions.

***E**arns the family's provision - breadwinner*

- He is responsible with the family's funds.
- He earns what is to be spent for the family.

***R**ests in God and is reassured by His word*

- His peace is from God.
- His understanding is from God.
- He constantly listens for God's voice of direction.
- His insight into situations is from God.

Judges 6:12 Joel 3:9-10
Copyright @ June 3, 2005

THE PROMISE

God is not a man that He should lie. Have you ever been promised something by someone you trusted, yet they failed to honour that promise? Have you ever made a promise that you did not honour? The Word says that we should not trust our flesh because it has the ability to fail.

The word says that God honours His word higher than His name and His word cannot return to Him void. When God created the heavens and the earth, He spoke and it came to pass. This reveals to us the power of God's spoken word, as He speaks creation is manifested. We were not made promises by God to have them fulfilled in our own strength.

We were given promises on the premise that He, God, holds the master plan. Our responsibility is to ensure that our hearts are prepared and ready for the fulfillment of those promises in our lives. Hold Him to every promise spoken because it must come to pass. Failure with God is impossible because His promises are orchestrated and executed by Him. Hold Him to His promises because they never fail.

THE PROMISE

The Lord has spoken into your spirit
He has defined His plans within your heart
He has predestined your life
He has orchestrated your path

You allow Him to prepare your spirit
You receive His promises with joy
A seed called 'promise' has been planted
Then you wait as a pregnant mother awaits the arrival of her baby

You allow the Lord to nourish your promise
To feed it exactly what it needs
Labour is long, labour is painful, labour is risky
Yet you push and you wait and you bear the pain.
And you push and wait and bear the pain
Yet nothing happens

Though the vision tarry wait for it
For He will watch over His word to perform it
Where is the promise?
Where is the blessing?

Where is the spiritual baby?
But is He a man that He should lie?
Can His word return void?
When He has spoken who can reverse it?
Regardless of the time span between the spoken
word and its manifestation
He is the Alpha and the Omega
He is the beginning and the end
He is the First and He is the Last
When He works who can reverse it?

He has set your destiny in the hands of eternity
Wait upon the Lord
Stand still and see the Salvation of the Lord

The promise has been spoken
The promise has been released
He spoke into you a promise
He did not speak into you a time frame
Hold fast to the Knowledge and Wisdom of God
Because His word must come to pass
It must perform what it was sent to do
Can the word return to God barren?

Impossible
The Promise Prevails!!!!!!!!

2 Chronicles 20:17 Isaiah 43:13, 44:6

Jeremiah 1:4 - 5 Habakkuk 2:3

Revelation 1:8

Copyright @ July 23, 2005

BROKEN... YET STILL CHOSEN

The path that the Lord predestines for you is one which you yourself were not and will never be consulted about. Your steps are ordered because you are righteous. Everything has purpose, and in purpose is destiny. Situations will come upon us in life and will attempt to derail our faith in God. But by building a firm foundation in Christ we will learn to stand on His word.

We can be broken by relationships, family, jobs, perceptions...but one thing that is sure is the hand of God upon us as we are chosen vessels to bring Him glory. We cannot determine what our path in life will be. Some are anointed to lead and some are anointed to follow, yet we are all chosen...... yes, often times broken but still chosen.

He promises to never leave us nor forsake us and His word is one incapable of returning void. Though we are bruised and then become broken we are led by Him in His infinite wisdom. Many times we feel out of place and out of destiny through brokenness and we are prompted by our own weaknesses to abort our calling. But God did not make a way for you to walk away. His plans must come to pass and to whom much is given much is required. We are often broken yet we are still chosen.

BROKEN...YET STILL CHOSEN

I am so broken

I am so battered

I am so bruised

Yet God still has a plan – I am chosen

A plan I cannot see

A plan I cannot even dream

My spirit is so worn

Areas in my life are so torn

Yet God still has a plan – I am chosen

I cannot see my way

I cannot take my place

Because I am not sure what it entails

I am so uncertain

Yet God still has a plan – I am chosen

My mind is bombarded with the wiles of this world

My spirit is so weak

My hope is so faint and bleak
I understand nothing that is happening
I am not sure how to feel
Yet God still has a plan – I am chosen

I don't like where I am
I pray the pain could end
I pray and fight and pray and fight
I sing and dance and sing and dance
Despite the things that get me down
I am clueless as to where my path is bound
I have no picture in my mind of my destiny
Yet I follow with my heart to eternity

Though my will stands strong
God breaks it to His
My heart is molded
My mind is transformed
Because He has a plan for my brokenness
Broken battered bruised by life
Yet open available to be used by God
Broken yet still chosen
My life has to be a witness

POETIC EXPERIENCES WITH GOD: From The Throne Room

When I am down to nothing
God is up to everything
I am great by His Spirit
I am holy by His Spirit
I am righteous through His Spirit
I am the Lord's
The devil has no foothold, no stronghold
No hold over my life

I am more than a conqueror through Christ Jesus
My smile is from the Lord
My joy within was hand delivered to me by Him
I never thought another smile could come forth
Feeling hopeless, faithless, useless
My life really has to stand out
To those I don't even know are watching
I cannot give up now
I just cannot let go

How many will I encourage to continue the road, I don't know.
I have to press forward
Press forward toward the prize

Never looking behind for there is a higher calling
God has a great plan for me
To use me to show others their destiny
Out of my brokenness
He sees His hand
Could my life ever fulfill any plan?

This life full of pain and sorrow
This life that seems like it has no tomorrow
A life full of bumps I never planned for
Could this life ever minister to any soul?
Never you ever give up because
God always has your purpose in His hand
Broken……. Yet Still Chosen…

Psalm 51:17 Matthew 22:14 John 15:16, 19
Copyright @ June 2, 2005

YOU ARE MY SHIELD

Have you ever had someone you could turn to who would protect you from all the bullies? Have you ever had things and situations come at you in life that you know you need to be protected from. Well the Lord is our shield.

Situations will always come against us in life once we have proclaimed Jesus as our Lord and Saviour but His word says He is our shield and buckler. He is our refuge and our strength. He is our ever present help in times of trouble. He leads and directs. He guides and protects. He shields.

A shield protects you from what would have harmed you, distracted you, and caused you to stumble or even destroy you. This shield is who God is in the present day world. He is the one who provides shelter and He is the one who provides refuge in every storm in our lives. When we feel as if we have lost the battle the Lord allows us to win them all. We are always victors and we always triumph by His word. You oh Lord are my shield.

YOU ARE MY SHIELD

You oh Lord are my shield
You are my shield against fear
You are my shield against the enemy
For you oh Lord are my shield
Though I walk through the valley of the shadow of death
You are my shield

When I walk away from you boldly in my own will
You are my shield
When I make decisions based on my own fleshly desires
You are my shield
When I am buffeted by the winds and waves of life
You are my shield

When I cannot see my way
When I don't know the right things to say
You are my shield

When everything seems so unfair
When nothing seems to bring good cheer
You are my shield

When the penetrating claws of sickness buffet my body
And the pangs of death draw ever near
You are my shield
When I lose the one that is very dear
You oh Lord are my shield

When the torturers pursue my every move
When my financial commitments are constantly unmoved
Even though I never know what awaits me
You are my shield
And you make my feet like those of a deer
You set me on a high place

Your truth is always near, hidden in my heart
You equip me with the shield of faith
Which protects me from the fiery darts of the enemy

POETIC EXPERIENCES WITH GOD: From The Throne Room

The darts of destruction, pain, sorrow, insecurity,
hopelessness, uncertainty and death
You are my shield oh God
You are my buckler

You are my strength
You are the one in whom I rest
You are the one in whom I live
You are the one in whom I have my being

You are the one who truly protects me
Even when I have drifted
You surround me with your shield of love
Oh Lord my God
You are my shield, my strength, my fortress, my refuge
You are my shield

Genesis 15:1 2 Samuel 22:31
Psalm 18:2 Psalm 28:7 Psalm 84:11
Copyright @ July 23, 2005

POETIC EXPERIENCES WITH GOD: From The Throne Room

POETIC EXPERIENCES WITH GOD: From The Throne Room

THE INNER LIGHT GLOWS

Sorrow and pain will come and they will go, usually unannounced. Sadness and depression can creep up on you like a literal thief in the night, coming to kill, steal and destroy. Things will come your way and you will not know what to do or say…..but God.

You will sometimes, as a child of God: get to your lowest point but rest assured that even in the darkest hour you must find something deep inside that will rise. As I learnt more about the Lord the enemy would try to afflict my mind with the worries of the world. Darkness tried to overpower me by trying to drive fear and intimidation into my spirit.

As low as I felt during the ordeal there was something deep within that rose up and rebuked that force even when my flesh was weak and worn. Out of my depression, out of my hopelessness, out of my loneliness an inner light that represents the light of God shone through the darkness with a mighty piercing force to be reckoned with.

The spirit of darkness fled and the child of light arose. Let your inner light shine for all men to see and when they look upon you and see your works they will glorify your Father. But we have this treasure in earthen vessels that the excellence of the power may be of God and not of us…..2 Corinthians 4:7.

"Let Your Inner Light Glow"!

THE INNER LIGHT GLOWS

Deep, dark, timeless
Senseless, speechless
Effortless, nothingness, blackness

No life form, no motivation, endless pain steps in.
Yet from deep within
Out of nothing, seems like nowhere
From the recesses of your Spirit comes a wave
A hope, which cries out
A flint, a spark
A light begins to glow through

Your Spirit rises
The spirit of death flees
The Spirit of light dwells
It infiltrates your very thoughts
It infiltrates your entire being
It circulates and gives life
It restores hope
It reassures confidence

Your inner light glows
Let your inner light glow!!!!

Proverbs 13:9 Matthew 5:14-16

Ephesians 5:8 1 Corinthians 6:20

Copyright @ March 25, 2004

WATCH YOUR WORDS......FOR YOUR WORDS WATCH YOU!!!!

That small thing can be so hard to keep in obedience, so difficult to keep in alignment with the word of God. Although you are a child of light you sometimes operate in darkness by your words. That small thing called the tongue. It says whatever comes to it without rationalizing the effects of what is spoken.

It can praise very highly one minute, and the next it speaks the deepest and vilest of curses. It is deadly by nature because our tendency is to sin. But by the Spirit it can be controlled. As we live, we live by faith and faith comes by hearing. So, if we are expressing evil thoughts then they will begin to manifest in our lives.

Whatever we say is uttered from our lips into the realm of the spirit. It is a seed planted waiting for the right moment to be harvested. It then sits in the realm of the spirit and waits on the respective forces to allow the words to manifest whether the spirit of light or the spirit of darkness. The negative words also wait for the right moment in time to manifest which is usually a spiritually weak moment. Then in the most unexpected moment the very words you had spoken overtake you and define your circumstances as well as order your steps. If your words were positive then positivity will manifest, if your words were negative then negativity will manifest.

There was a period in my life when negative things would keep happening and the Spirit of the Lord revealed it to me that my negatively spoken words have the power to influence my season. He took me through a verbal cleansing and this was how my life took a positive turn as He taught me how to enter His rest by my positive utterances.

Life and death are in the power of the tongue. Watch your words for your words watch you.

What you say will make the way, for what you say to be your way. James 1:26, James 3:1 – 12.

WATCH YOUR WORDS...FOR YOUR WORDS WATCH YOU!!!!

What you say, will make the way,
For what you say, to be your way

What you speak is what you will have because life and death are in the power of the tongue. Whoever guards his mouth and tongue keeps his soul from troubles. Watch your words and hold your tongue, you will save yourself a lot of grief.
Proverbs 21:23 (Message)

SPEAK LIFE, PROPHESY BY THE SPIRIT AND WATCH THE LORD WORK!!

Always ensure that your words are soft, gentle and seasoned by the Holy Spirit because you might have to eat them, so ensure they are palatable.
Remember criticism is a manifestation of pride

and we know what the word of God reveals about this.

Pride goes before destruction and a haughty spirit before a fall.

(Proverbs 16:18 NKJV Spirit Filled)

First pride, then the crash, the bigger the ego, the harder the fall.

(Proverbs 16:18 Message)

A man's pride will bring him low, but the humble in spirit will retain honour

(Proverbs 29:23 NKJV Spirit filled)

Pride lands you flat on your face; humility prepares you for honours. (Proverbs 29:23 Message)

Always watch your words ...for your words watch you!!!

Ezekiel 37: 1-14

Copyright @ March 31, 2005

SPEAK LIFE

The words that you speak
Determine if you are strong or weak
The things that you say
Will make the way for what you say to be your way
Be watchful over that small one (the tongue)

It can make your worries prolong
Longer than you can bear
Because with your ill words you tear
Your destiny to pieces
By speaking a negative thesis
Over your steps that should be ordered

So small yet so powerful
Very difficult to tame
So strong the words that are uttered
Never allowing you to remain the same

The spoken words frame your life
It can release love, it can cause strife
It can radiate peace, it can speak life

It can set your heart at ease
Speak only what you hear the Holy Spirit release
Ensure it is to holiness that you tune your ear
For His voice will guide you out of fear
His voice is reassuring that He is always near

Speak in authority never doubting whatever He says
Speak with boldness and speak life
Speak life into a dead situation
Speak life into your financial stagnation
Speak life into your broken marriage
Speak life into your constant worries

Speak life that you will overcome
Speak life that His Kingdom will come
Speak life so you will live and not die
Speak life according to His word that cannot lie
Speak peace, speak prosperity, speak into your destiny

Speak yourself out of your present state
Even though to you it may seem late

Speak and let your words frame your path
For silence will only remain a thought
Bless the Lord with the fruit of your lips
Allow the Holy Spirit to give you spiritual tips

For what you say will make the way
For what you say to be your way
Speak life, for life and death are in the power of the tongue.

Job 27:4 Psalm 12:4, 120:2, 139:4
Proverbs 15:4
Copyright © May 30, 2007

MANIFEST

Speak life and you will receive life. Speak death and you will receive death. Whatever you believe, whatever you perceive, whatever you confess will manifest. The promises of God are Yea and Amen and whatever He has ordered over your life will manifest. Whatever God has started He is faithful to bring it to completion. It is natural for us to speak ill of situations in our lives and not declare the word of the Lord.

Remember, life and death are in the power of the tongue so whatever you verbalize will linger in the spirit until the perfect environment allows it to manifest in the natural.

Your life must speak volumes when the Glory of God becomes manifested in it. It is not by might, nor by power, but it is by the spirit of the living God that destiny is fulfilled in your life. God's divine plan for you has already been set in eternity and it will be manifested by His grace.

The manifestation of our purpose cannot be earned but is given only by God. Call all promises over your life to manifest so you can walk boldly into your destiny.

MANIFEST

The Lord has released my destiny to me
My life is evidence of His Glory
The Lord has prepared my life from before the foundations of the earth
And He has given to me my ordered steps
I will see all the things that will come forth because He has ordained it

The Lord has lifted the banner of delay from over my life
And I am walking in my prophetic destiny
I am fulfilling the purpose of God in my life
My manifested all has been given to me
And I will praise the Lord all my days

The Lord has given me His right hand
He has touched the broken areas of my life and mended it into destiny
The Lord has called me by name and spoken who I am
The Lord has given unto me His favour and blessed me beyond measure

My life will reflect the blessings of the Lord
because I am obedient to His word
There shall be no forced hand in my life because
my steps are ordered by God

His Glory shall fill my house for I am His child
His Glory will be manifested in my life
Manifest, manifest, manifest, manifest, call all
things to life
I will give God the Glory with my life
My ways shall demonstrate the will of God

I will not turn away from the Lord
Because He is my rock, my fortress, my strength
and my deliverer
The Lord will be delighted by my ways
My life shall give birth to purpose

Manifest, manifest, manifest, manifest
Call all things to life
Manifest

Psalm 18:1, 27:1, 28:8   John 14:21
Copyright © September 27, 2005

POETIC EXPERIENCES WITH GOD: From The Throne Room

EPILOGUE

Life is a journey and no one knows where the route will take you. Most times you know where you are going but have no idea how you will get there. The Lord knows the end from the beginning. Life's journey can take you up steep mountains that require your total strength, deep valleys that are easy to ride down but leaves you at the bottom, crooked paths with many craters and speed bumps that require your patience, and around some deep corners that you cannot see, but require your trust.

Wherever the journey of life takes you, God is with you. The seasons of life are very much alive and though we have no control over them, we must learn to embrace them with every level of understanding and guidance from above. If we learn to trust the hand that leads us into every season, we will always rise to the top in everything we do. Refrain from living life always having some selfish agenda because with that you will not get by and be filled with purpose.

Never live a life of regrets and constantly looking back. It will stagnate your ability to move forward, stump your growth and take your life. No one drives a car and stays focused in the rearview...if you do, it will show you what you have overcome (your past), but it will distract you from your destination (your future). Staring at your rearview (your past) will inevitably take your future from your grasp.

Never live a life of regret because your past is what shaped you into who you are today but it doesn't mean you should live there. Get up, stand up, rise up and walk into your future that God holds. God never makes mistakes.

The Birthing, The Flourishing, The Breaking and The Living, represent a perpetual cycle just like the very seasons of nature, transitioning through inevitable change. Change that we are sometimes prepared for and change that sometimes takes us by surprise.

To truly appreciate your present, you have to learn from your past season, not dwell there and allow it to keep you stagnant but learn from it so it can propel you into your future. Your past serves the purpose of guiding you away from repeating the same mistakes.

The steps of a righteous man are ordered. No retreat, no surrendering to that which is behind but pressing toward the mark of the high calling of God. He knows the end from the beginning. Your latter will be greater; your best is yet to come. What the enemy meant for bad the Lord will turn it for your good.

Believe God and watch Him work on your behalf.

POETIC EXPERIENCES WITH GOD: From The Throne Room

NOTES

POETIC EXPERIENCES WITH GOD: From The Throne Room

www.ingramcontent.com/pod-product-compliance
Lightning Source LLC
Chambersburg PA
CBHW041620220426
43661CB00049B/1549